From the desktop of Jeffrey Simmons

A vacation in Paris inspired Miroslav Sasek to create childrens travel guides to the big cities of the world. He brought me *This is Paris* in 1958 when I was publishing in London, and we soon followed up with *This is London.* Both books were enormously successful, and his simple vision grew to include more than a dozen books. Their amusing verse, coupled with bright and charming illustrations, made for a series unlike any other, and garnered Sasek (as we always called him) the international and popular acclaim he deserved.

I was thrilled to learn that *This is Britain* will once again find its rightful place on book-shelves. Sasek is no longer with us (and I have lost all contact with his family), but I am sure he would be delighted to know that a whole new generation of wide-eyed readers is being introduced to his whimsical, imaginative, and enchanting world.

Your name here

Published by arrangement with Simon & Schuster Books for Young Readers,
Simon & Schuster Children's Publishing Division

This edition first published in the United States of America in 2008 by
UNIVERSE PUBLISHING
A Division of Rizzoli International Publications, Inc.
300 Park Avenue South
New York, NY 10010
www.rizzoliusa.com

2009 2010 2011 2012 / 10 9 8 7 6 5 4 3 2

Printed in China

ISBN-10: 0-7893-1753-2
ISBN-13: 978-0-7893-1753-7

Library of Congress Control Number: 2007934238

Cover design: centerpointdesign

There's such a lot to see, but we've got to start somewhere — so let's start at the Tower of London by the River Thames. Inside you can see the Crown Jewels, the Beefeaters, and the ravens.

6

On the right is Tower Bridge, which divides to let tall ships go through.

When the Royal Standard is flying over Buckingham Palace it means the Queen is in residence. Crowds gather outside the railings each day to watch the Changing of the Guard.

Westminster Abbey is London's most important church. Beyond it you can see the two towers of the Houses of Parliament — on the left, the Clock Tower with Big Ben, and on the right, the Victoria Tower . . .

. . . and here are the Houses of Parliament themselves — on the left, the Lords, and on the right, the Commons. This is where the country's laws are passed. You can go inside and watch it happening.

St. Paul's Cathedral is in the City of London. Some think it is the most beautiful church in London. Just down the road is Fleet Street, where most of Britain's national newspapers are published.* Leading off Fleet Street there are many little alleys and courts dating back to the seventeenth century. Many of them are associated with Dr. Johnson. He lived in three of them, and in one of them, Wine Office Court, is Ye Olde Cheshire Cheese, a pub where he and James Boswell used to meet.

The center of London is the West End — and the very center is Piccadilly Circus. Most of the big theaters, cinemas, and shops are a short walk from here . . .

. . . and so is Trafalgar Square, where Admiral
Nelson presides over the lions and pigeons
from the top of his column.

A short train — or boat — ride from London, and here we are at Hampton Court, Henry VIII's palace by the Thames. Don't get lost in the maze! Henry used to hunt in the forests around it and you can still see herds of deer in nearby Richmond Park. Less wild are the botanical gardens of Kew, just down the river.

Woburn Abbey is the home of the Duke of Bedford. As you can see it's very handsome. The 3,000-acre estate also has a wildlife park. Queen Elizabeth I visited the abbey in 1572, but the Earl of Bedford hoped she would stay no more than a day and two nights.

And this is Windsor Castle, another royal palace, set in a pretty country town. The view from the Round Tower is said to include twelve counties. English kings and queens have lived in the castle since the eleventh century. Here is Castle Hill . . .

. . . and here is another view of Windsor Castle, this time from the Thames. On the opposite side of the river from the castle is Eton village with its famous school, founded in 1440. Further down the river, a short distance from Windsor, are the Runnymede meadows where, on the 15th of June 1215, King John reluctantly signed the Magna Carta. The Kennedy Memorial is in the same field.

This little crooked house in Windsor is called Market Cross House. It was bought in 1656 for £82 ($20,000 today) by one William Bradbury. Beside it is the Guildhall, built by Sir Christopher Wren, who designed St. Paul's Cathedral.

Oxford is the second oldest university in Europe. This college, Christ Church, was founded in 1524 by Cardinal Wolsey. We are in its main square, Tom Quad (short for quadrangle), facing Tom Tower.

Corpus Christi College is older — it was started in 1517. It is one of the smaller colleges. We can't see any of the undergraduates (the students) in their black gowns; they must be on vacation.

Mob Quad, in Merton College, dates back to the Middle Ages, as far as 1264, in fact. The university at Oxford was probably first started when Henry II banned English students from attending the University of Paris.

The Bodleian Library is one of the oldest in the world. It is full of many rare manuscripts and books.

No tour of Britain would be complete without a visit to Shakespeare's
town of Stratford-upon-Avon. This is the house where he was born.
It is still perfectly preserved . . .

. . . and so is New Place,
which is not new at all, and
where he died. There are
lots of other lovely Tudor
houses in Stratford such
as Hall's croft where John
Hall, Shakespeare's son-in-
law, lived. Stratford is much
older than Shakespeare's
time though; people have
lived there since the
Bronze Age.

The Holy Trinity Church, where Shakespeare was buried . . .

. . . and his memorial, inside the church.

Here is the home of John Harvard's mother — he was the founder of America's Harvard University.

This is Chester Cathedral. Chester is a very old town. In "the Rows" the medieval houses have an overhanging first floor, converting the narrow road into a shady corridor. Not far away, in the village of Neston, the future Lady Hamilton grew up in poverty, later to become Horatio Nelson's mistress and one of the most famous women of her time.

From this tower Charles I watched the progress of his troops in the Battle of Rowton Moor. It has since been named King Charles's Tower.

There are quite a few black-and-white herringbone half-timbered houses like this in Cheshire. This one is Little Moreton Hall. Not far away is Knutsford, the town immortalized by Mrs. Gaskell in her novel *Cranford*. We are still in Cheshire, but only a little way north is the River Mersey and Liverpool, in Lancashire, where The Beatles came from.

Carlisle Castle is one of a series of medieval fortresses on the border built to defend the English against the Scots. It did not fall until 1745, when Bonnie Prince Charlie rode into Carlisle on a white horse with a hundred pipers marching in front of him. But before long he was on his way home to Scotland after being beaten by the English at Derby.

Hadrian's Wall was built by the Romans, also to keep the Scots out of Britain. Originally it ran from Carlisle in the west to Newcastle in the east, and much of it is still standing.

The whole town of Durham was once confined to a bend in the River Wear that doubles back on itself, nearly making a small island. You can see the old town, with the cathedral and castle on the other side of the bridge in the picture. Now much of the old town has been taken over by the university, and the great hall of the castle is the students' dining room.

Yorkshire, the largest county in England, is famous for its moors, its pudding, and the city of York, whose principal church is called the Minster.* Here it is. It has a very famous stained-glass window called the Five Sisters. The whole building took two and a half centuries to complete. Not far away, near the River Ouse, is the site of one of the major battles of the First English Civil War — Marston Moor.

York is one of many British cities whose ancient outer
walls have survived. In the York Castle Museum you can
see life-size reconstructions of old York streets complete
with shops, vehicles, and people. You can also drive out onto
the famous Yorkshire moors to Brontë country
and visit the sisters' old home in Haworth, near Keighley —
now a museum.

Lincoln Cathedral contains one of only four remaining original copies of the Magna Carta. In the town there is a castle founded by William the Conqueror and a gateway that has been in use since Roman times. Not very far away is Somersby, where Tennyson was born, and Grantham, where Isaac Newton went to school. Near Lincoln is the town of Boston, after which Boston in Massachusetts was named.

Ely Cathedral is one of the major monuments of East Anglia. You can see it for miles around because the countryside is so flat. It is in the Isle of Ely, which isn't an island at all, but a part of Cambridgeshire.

The house in Ely where Oliver Cromwell, leader of the Roundheads in the First English Civil War, lived from 1636 to 1647. Cromwell also had a farm in the village of Stuntney, a mile southeast of Ely. From this village you will find the very best view of the cathedral.

It would never do to mention Oxford and not Cambridge. After all, in the annual boat race between the two universities, Cambridge has won more times. This is Trinity College, and we are in the Great Court.

The President's Lodge at Queens' College. There are about 11,700 undergraduates in residence at Cambridge, some 500 more than at Oxford.

This is another college, the oldest in Cambridge. It's simply called Peterhouse.

Here is King's College. The white building in the middle is the College Chapel, which has a very famous choir.

Bury St. Edmunds is a beautiful Georgian town in Suffolk. This well-preserved gateway leads to the fourteenth-century abbey. You can just see the portcullis that they used to lower to keep out attackers. It's been a long time since anybody attacked the abbey, though.

The abbey itself is more of a romantic ruin. In the nearby Stour Valley John Constable painted many of his famous landscapes.

Not far from Bury is Colchester, the oldest recorded town in England. This is what's left of its Norman castle. There used to be water in the moat, but now you can stroll around in it. It was near here that Queen Boadicea led her army in revolt against the Romans.

At this spot Thomas Becket, the archbishop of Canterbury, was murdered in 1170 by four knights who mistakenly thought King Henry II wanted to get rid of him. Afterwards the king was very sorry, and the cathedral became a center for pilgrims from all over Europe. Chaucer's *Canterbury Tales* is about a group of these pilgrims telling each other stories on their way to St. Thomas's shrine.

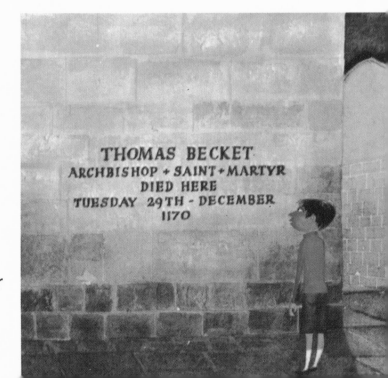

THOMAS BECKET
ARCHBISHOP + SAINT + MARTYR
DIED HERE
TUESDAY 29TH - DECEMBER
1170

Opposite is Canterbury Cathedral. Canterbury is the county town of Kent. All over the county you will see field after field of hops, used for making beer, and the oast houses in which the hops are dried. This is one of the reasons why Kent is known as the Garden of England. In the western part of the county is Chartwell, Sir Winston Churchill's beautiful Tudor home, now a museum.

The West Gate of Canterbury has hardly altered in the last six hundred years. One addition is a museum inside it.

There is also an abbey at Canterbury. It was founded by St. Augustine and is outside the city walls. Until the death of St. Thomas Becket it was more important than the cathedral.

Brighton in Sussex is the best known of the many English seaside resorts. It has miles of beaches and a dolphinarium, a sort of circus with dolphins, and lovely Regency buildings.* Until 1724 Brighton was just a small fishing town. Then sea-bathing became fashionable, and in 1820 the Prince Regent built this extraordinary palace, the Royal Pavilion, and took his court to Brighton.

Dover is the nearest English town to France. On a clear day you can see the French coast from these cliffs — the famous White Cliffs of Dover. Dover used to be the chief of the "Cinque Ports." There is a Norman castle overlooking the sea with the remains of a Roman lighthouse inside its grounds.

Salisbury has the tallest cathedral in Britain. It was built in the thirteenth century and the spire is 404 feet high. Unfortunately the foundations were not strong enough to take so great a weight. In the library there is a report from Sir Christopher Wren, the seventeenth-century architect, on the condition of the spire.

Salisbury Plain contains another remarkable monument — the circle of gigantic stones known as Stonehenge. Construction began nearly five thousand years ago. Nobody quite knows why it was built; perhaps as a huge astronomical instrument to calculate the movement of the sun, or perhaps as a place for sun worship. Despite their enormous size the stones were brought all the way from Wales and are very accurately placed. Stonehenge, and the nearby Avebury Ring, are full of mysteries. Bronze Age axes that have been found on the site are similar to some discovered at prehistoric Mycenae in Greece. How did they get there?

And now we're in the West Country. Devon is famous for its cream and its sailors. The pilgrim fathers sailed to America from Plymouth on the *Mayflower*, and on the Hoe (a grassy public space) in Plymouth, Sir Francis Drake supposedly played bowls while the Spanish Armada approached. Exeter is the capital of Devon. It is a very old town, first founded by the Romans. The picture shows Exeter Cathedral; two of its towers were built in 1050, but the rest is a little more modern. In the Cathedral Close there is a shop which used to be Mol's Coffee House, where it is said that Drake, his fellow navigator Sir John Hawkins, and others used to meet.

And this is the Guildhall, built in the fifteenth century. Underneath Exeter are medieval passages constructed over streams that used to provide the town with a constant supply of fresh spring water.

Wells Cathedral in Somerset, the "cider country." Inside the
cathedral there is a remarkable fourteenth-century clock, across
whose face knights joust on the striking of the hours.* Nearby is
the thirteenth-century Bishop's Palace, where the swans in the
moat ring a bell near the drawbridge when they are hungry.
Wells shares its bishop with Bath . . .

. . . which is named after these Roman baths, built over a natural spring of hot water. People have been coming here for nearly a thousand years to cure their ailments in the waters. The Roman town was called Aquae Sulis, but another town grew up in its place and the Roman baths weren't rediscovered until the nineteenth century. Eighteenth-century Bath grew into a spa — a fashionable society resort — and many streets of beautiful houses were built, some in a perfect curve, like the Royal Crescent. Behind the baths in the picture you can see the abbey.

Bristol has a long history as a seaport and many explorers and merchants started their voyages from there. Among them was John Cabot, who sailed from Bristol in 1497 and discovered the mainland of North America, landing in Newfoundland, Canada. For his discovery he was paid the princely sum of £10 and a £20-a-year pension by Henry VII ($11,500 and $19,000 today). The hundred-foot Cabot Tower in the picture was named after him.

Many of Bristol's medieval and renaissance buildings were destroyed during World War II. Among the survivors is this pub, the Llandoger Trow ("trow" means barge), built in 1664. It is said that it was here that Daniel Defoe first heard the story he turned into *Robinson Crusoe*, and also that Robert Louis Stevenson used it as the setting for part of *Treasure Island*. In the same street you can see the famous Theatre Royal, which was built in 1766 and is probably the oldest playhouse still in use in this country.

The town of Gloucester began as a Roman fort. Many of the streets still follow the old Roman roads. It was in Gloucester that William the Conqueror decided to make the survey of England known as the *Domesday Book*. This is the eleventh-century cathedral with its 225-foot pinnacled tower. Inside is the medieval Great Peter Bell, which weighs three tons.

This is Tewkesbury Cathedral. Near here one of the bloodiest battles in the Wars of the Roses was fought, and the site is still known as Bloody Meadow. Tewkesbury has a great many old houses and half-timbered inns. Among them is the Royal Hop Pole, before whose fourteenth-century fireplace Dickens's character Mr. Pickwick warmed himself and ate such a large meal that he slept for the next thirty miles of his journey.

Another of the sights of Tewkesbury is this fine old mill. From its windows you can look across at the outer walls of the abbey buildings and at the monks' granary.

There has been a church on the site of Hereford Cathedral since 825. In Hereford's marketplace in 1802, a man auctioned off his wife for £1 4s ($158 today) and a bowl of punch!

Mappa Mundi is Latin for map of the world. This one, in Hereford Cathedral, shows the world as it was thought to be in the thirteenth century — flat. Much of the world, including America, had not been charted then.

King Stephen was supposed to have sat in this chair. He reigned over England — rather inefficiently — during the first half of the twelfth century.

This is Wales! There are lots of castles in this small country. This one is at Cardiff. It is Norman, but it's hidden behind a facade designed by a Victorian architect, William Burges, when it was the home of the Marquess of Bute. Cardiff itself is an old seaport, and through the ages it has always been full of sailors, including parties of pirates who used to come ashore and frighten the townsfolk. Now Cardiff is the quiet principal city of Wales, and there are no more pirates.

But there is a Welsh Folk Museum at nearby St. Fagan's, where there are assembled objects recalling Welsh life in the past, even including complete buildings brought in pieces and reassembled.

Tintern Abbey, on the River Wye, was founded in 1131 but was dissolved by Henry VIII, and only some of the buildings still stand. Looking down on the abbey from the hills, William Wordsworth was so impressed by the beauty of the scene that he wrote a poem about it.

Monmouth is a border town and it has always been disputed whether it belongs to England or Wales.* The Monnow Bridge, built in 1272, has a fortified gatehouse. It was used for collecting tolls — three pence ($7 today) for every ship laden with goods for sale in Monmouth, and four pence ($10 today) for every bag of wool.

Monmouth is especially famous for two people: King Henry V, victor of the Battle of Agincourt, and the Honorable Charles Stewart Rolls, co-founder of the Rolls-Royce motor car company and the first man to fly across the English Channel both ways. Both are commemorated by statues in front of the eighteenth-century Shire Hall. Henry V is in a niche on the wall below the clock, and Rolls has a pedestal in the square.

This is Conway Castle, known in Welsh as Aberconwy. The old town is still contained within its medieval walls and the castle still stands much as it did in 1295, when King Edward I, who built the castle, was besieged by the Welsh under Llywelyn, the last of the independent Welsh princes.

Conway claims to have the oldest house in Wales, and also the smallest house in Britain — this sixteenth-century fisherman's cottage on the quay. It is 72 inches wide and 122 inches high, and has two tiny rooms and a staircase.

Caernarvon is where the investiture of the Prince of Wales is held, because it was in this castle that Edward I presented his newborn son to the Welsh after he had killed their Prince Llywelyn in battle. Prince Charles was made Prince of Wales here by the Queen in 1969. This is Castle Square . . .

. . . and this is what the castle looks like from the other side. It was built by Edward I to help keep his hold on Wales. The area enclosed by the castle walls is three acres and the walls themselves are twenty feet thick at their base. A short drive from Caernarvon is Portmeirion, a village created by the architect Clough Williams-Ellis to show that new buildings don't have to disfigure the countryside. His gaily colored, unusually shaped houses nestle prettily on the edges of hills and behind trees.

Harlech Castle is yet another of Edward I's Welsh castles. It was completed in 1290. In the Wars of the Roses it was the last stronghold of the Lancastrians. Margaret of Anjou fled there after their defeat by the Yorkists.

Pembroke Castle, just outside the port of Milford Haven. It is surrounded on three sides by the tides of the Haven (or harbor). Henry Tudor grew up in the castle before he was exiled to Brittany. In 1485 he returned there before the Battle of Bosworth in which he defeated Richard III and gained the crown of England, as Henry VII.

And this is Scotland! Edinburgh Castle, surrounded by the rambling streets of the old town, sits high above the new town and the surrounding lowland on a large piece of volcanic rock. Perched at the very top is St. Margaret's Chapel, which is only large enough to hold twenty-five people. The kings and queens of Scotland lived in the castle.* It was here, in a tiny room, that Mary Queen of Scots gave birth to James I.

From outside the castle the Royal Mile leads down a fascinating street full of ancient houses, dark courtyards, and narrow, curving stone stairways to the royal Palace of Holyroodhouse. It was not until the reign of James IV that the official palace was built, next to a very old abbey, and in 1543 it was largely destroyed by fire during an English invasion. Mary Queen of Scots lived in the remaining part of the house, and here, in a room you can still visit, her secretary Rizzio was murdered.

Linlithgow Palace in West Lothian is one of Scotland's four royal palaces. James V and Mary Queen of Scots were born here.

Here is Braemar Castle, built on a knoll above the River Dee. It was started in 1628 but has been much altered since then. Every September at Braemar are held the Highland Games, known as "the Gathering." It is famous all over the world and the Queen always attends.

Balmoral Castle in Aberdeenshire, the personal holiday home of the Queen. It was built for Queen Victoria and she spent much of her time here. She called it "my dear paradise." One of her favorite views was at Killiecrankie on Loch Tommel, now known as "Queen's View."

Stirling Castle is in a very important position on the road to the Highlands, and during wars it always became a center of fighting. The famous Battle of Bannockburn in 1314 was fought over it. There was much fighting between the English and the Scots before they were united. In Inverness you can visit the site of the Battle of Culloden, where the English and the Campbells cruelly slaughtered the retreating Scots.

Fort William is not a fort but a town. It is on the east shore of Loch Linnhe, with Ben Nevis towering behind. There used to be a fort here but it was demolished in 1890 to make way for a railway. Ben Nevis is 4,409 feet high and is the highest mountain in the British Isles.

Scotland is full of beautiful long lochs. This is Loch Lomond. It is twenty-four miles long and the largest stretch of inland water in Great Britain. Many think it is also the most beautiful. There are a number of islands in the loch. One contains the ruins of an old castle; another is the burial place of the clan MacGregor.
Another loch in Scotland, Loch Ness, is supposed to contain an enormous monster. Many people say they have seen it, some even have a photograph of it, but no one can prove it exists.

This is Britain!

A Sasek Map of the World

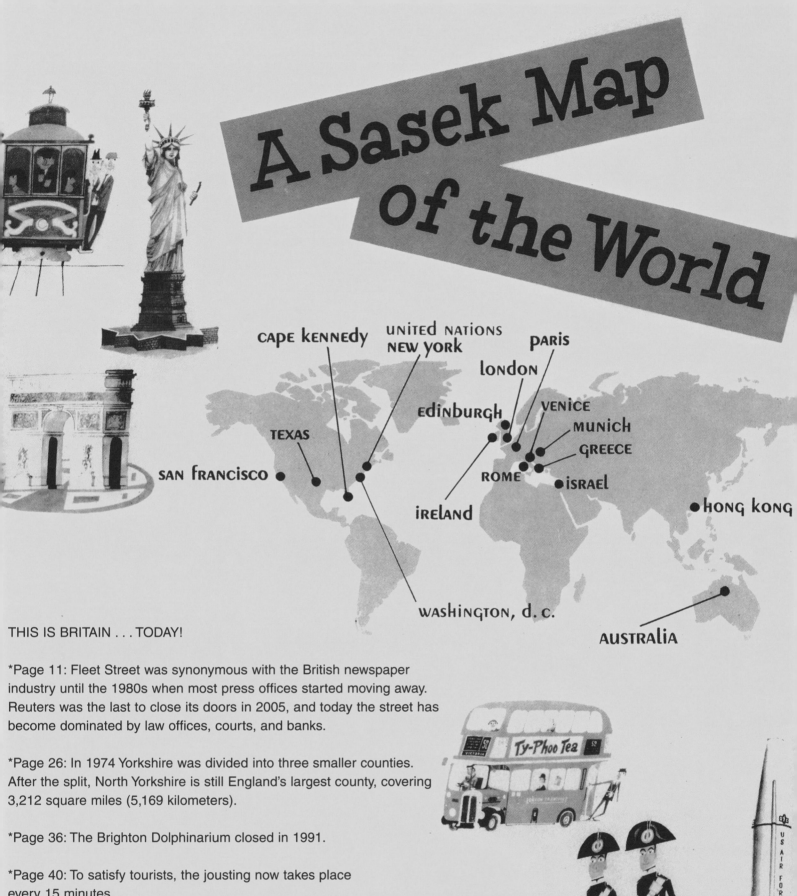

CAPE KENNEDY
UNITED NATIONS
NEW YORK
PARIS
LONDON
EDINBURGH
VENICE
MUNICH
GREECE
TEXAS
SAN FRANCISCO
ROME
ISRAEL
IRELAND
HONG KONG
WASHINGTON, D.C.
AUSTRALIA

THIS IS BRITAIN . . . TODAY!

*Page 11: Fleet Street was synonymous with the British newspaper industry until the 1980s when most press offices started moving away. Reuters was the last to close its doors in 2005, and today the street has become dominated by law offices, courts, and banks.

*Page 26: In 1974 Yorkshire was divided into three smaller counties. After the split, North Yorkshire is still England's largest county, covering 3,212 square miles (5,169 kilometers).

*Page 36: The Brighton Dolphinarium closed in 1991.

*Page 40: To satisfy tourists, the jousting now takes place every 15 minutes.

*Page 48: Historically, there has been a long-simmering debate over whether the county of Monmouthshire belongs to England or Wales, but since 1974 it has been placed definitively in Wales.

*Page 54: The kingdom of Scotland merged with the kingdom of England in 1707 to become the kingdom of Great Britain. They have been united under a single monarch ever since.